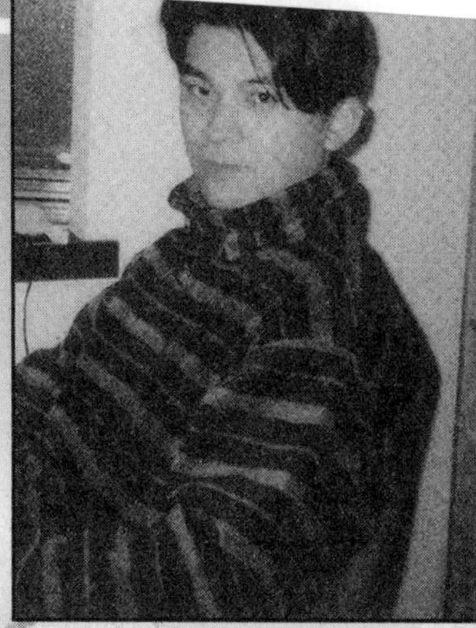

Name: Takeshi Konomi
Profile: Two years ago...

"Phew! It's been about six months since The Prince of Tennis started, and it's all finally coming together! But I do wish an anime, a video game, and trading cards would result from it. I guess that's a difficult feat for a sports manga."

"What—it's already on sale over there? Just kidding...(weeping in gratitude)."

About Takeshi Konomi

Takeshi Konomi exploded onto the manga scene with the incredible **THE PRINCE OF TENNIS**. His refined art style and sleek character designs proved popular with **Weekly Shonen Jump** readers, and **THE PRINCE OF TENNIS** became the No. 1 sports manga in Japan almost overnight...

THE PRINCE OF TENNIS
VOL. 13
The SHONEN JUMP Manga

STORY AND ART BY
TAKESHI KONOMI

English Adaptation/Michelle Pangilinan
Translation/Joe Yamazaki
Touch-up Art & Lettering/Andy Ristaino
Graphics and Cover Design/Janet Piercy
Editor/Michelle Pangilinan

Managing Editor/Elizabeth Kawasaki
Director of Production/Noboru Watanabe
Vice President of Publishing/Alvin Lu
Vice President & Editor in Chief/ Yumi Hoashi
Sr. Director of Acquisitions/Rika Inouye
Vice President of Sales & Marketing/Liza Coppola
Publisher/Hyoe Narita

Printed in the U.S.A.

Published by VIZ Media, LLC
P.O. Box 77010
San Francisco, CA 94107

SHONEN JUMP Manga Edition
10 9 8 7 6 5 4 3 2 1
First printing, May 2006

Shonen Jump Manga

ENNIS CLUB

● TAKASHI KAWAMURA ● KUNIMITSU TEZUKA ● SHUICHIRO OISHI ● RYOMA ECHIZEN ●

STORY & CHARACTERS

Ryoma Echizen, a student at Seishun Academy, is a tennis prodigy who won four consecutive U.S. Junior tournaments. The first-ever 7th grade starter, Ryoma leads his team through to the District Preliminaries! Despite a few mishaps, Seishun advances to the finals of the City Tournament and plays Yamabuki Junior High School in the finals. The doubles pair of Shuichiro and Eiji struggles, but they avenge their loss from the previous year. Momo beats Kiyosumi as well! With a 2-1 win-loss record, Seishun's victory rests on Ryoma's shoulders once again! Ryoma meets a worthy opponent in Jin, another tennis prodigy, but will the latter's strength draw out the best in Ryoma?!

SEIGAKU TI

● KAORU KAIDO ● TAKESHI MOMOSHIRO ● SADAHARU INUI ● EIJI KIKUMARU ● SHUSUKE FUJI ●

SEISHUN ACADEMY TENNIS TEAM COACH

SUMIRE RYUZAKI

SEISHUN TENNIS TEAM

SAKUNO RYUZAKI

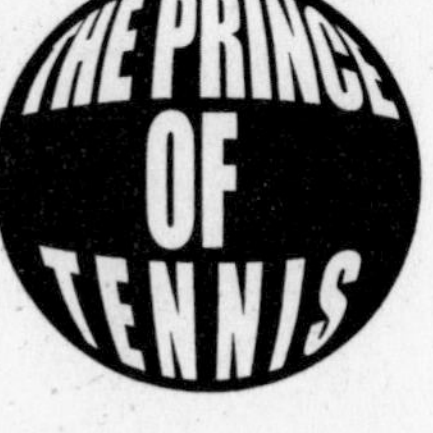

SEISHUN TENNIS TEAM

SATOSHI HORIO

SEISHUN TENNIS TEAM

KACHIRO KATO

SEISHUN TENNIS TEAM

KATSUO MIZUNO

YAMABUKI JUNIOR HIGH SCHOOL

JIN AKUTSU

YAMABUKI JUNIOR HIGH SCHOOL

TAICHI DAN

YAMABUKI JUNIOR HIGH SCHOOL

KIYOSUMI SENGOKU

CONTENTS

GENIUS 106:
UNBECOMING

TOKYO TOURNAMENT
(MENS GROUP)
THE CITY TOURNAMENT'S ALMOST OVER...
SEISHUN'S LEADING 2-1, HUH?
THEY'LL BE THE CHAMPS IF THEY WIN THE NO. 2 SINGLES MATCH.
JIN...
TUP

THERE'S A REASON WHY HE CAN'T POSSIBLY LOSE...

HMPH!
FSS
山吹中
RAA
HEY JIN!
THAT'S QUITE UNBE-COMING OF YOU!
RA

WHO DO YOU THINK YOU'RE TALKING TO, YOU OLD FART?
I'LL BASH YOUR HEAD IN!
KEKE
PFFT... YOU SOUND LIKE YOU STILL HAVE SOME ENERGY LEFT IN YOU.
KEKE

TWO MONTHS AGO AT YAMA-BUKI JUNIOR HIGH SCHOOL ...
HEH— TENNIS...
THIS IS SO FIVE YEARS AGO...

CLAP
CLAP
CLAP

CLAP
CLAP
CLAP
TRULY IMPRESSIVE!
AMAZING!
KE
KE
FWW
GRAB
WHO THE HECK ARE YOU? DON'T TOUCH ME!

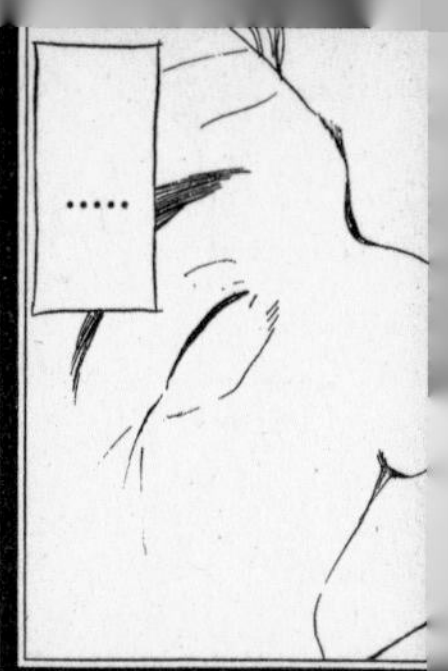
.....

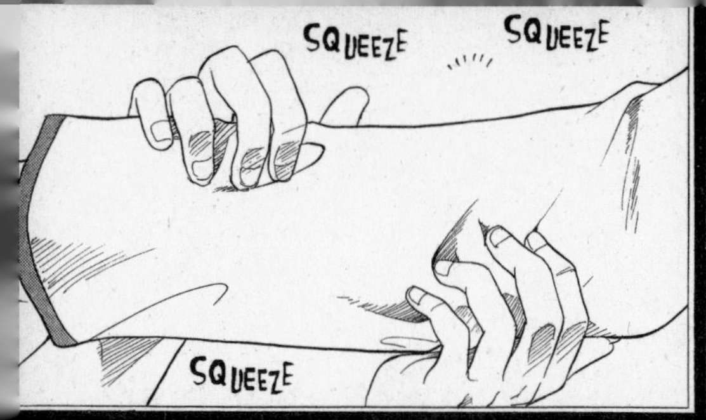
SQUEEZE
SQUEEZE
SQUEEZE

SOFT BUT FIRM...
COUGH
COUGH
GREAT MUSCLES WITH NO EXTRA FLAB...

?

KE KE

IF YOU DON'T BELONG TO ANY CLUB...
WANT TO GIVE THE TENNIS TEAM A WHIRL?
SHOES ALLOWED ON COURT...

TIME!
YAMA-BUKI!
YAMA-BUKI!
WAA
SEIS-HUN!
SEIS-HUN!

TRY THROWING OFF HIS RHYTHM...

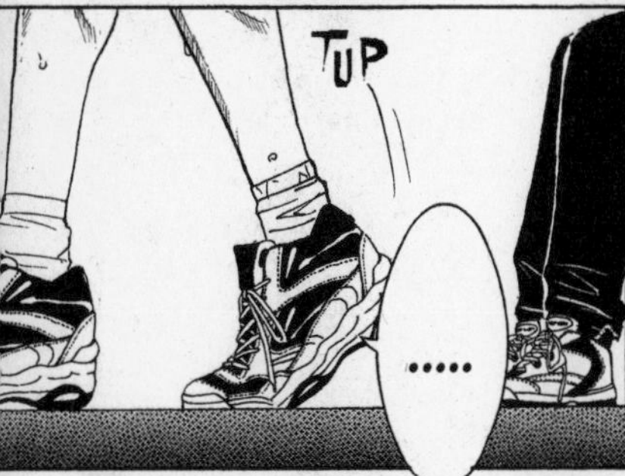

WAA
WHO DO YOU THINK YOU'RE TRYING TO COACH?

HAVE YOU FORGOTTEN WHO I AM...?

NOBODY STANDS A CHANCE AGAINST ME–

I'M JIN AKUTSU!!

I'VE CRUSHED EVERYONE WHO HAS GOTTEN IN MY WAY!

AND THAT'S NOT ABOUT TO CHANGE TODAY!!

WAAA
COACH RYUZAKI...

ANY PLAYER WHO PRAC-TICES HARD...
...AND GIVES IT THEIR ALL HAS NOTHING TO BE ASHAMED OF...
BUT A COCKY FELLOW WHO MOCKS THIS SPORT AND BARELY PRACTICES ...
...AND ENDS UP LOSING ...

WELL, THERE'S NOTHING MORE UNBE-COMING.

山吹中
THAT'S WHY HE WILL NEVER ALLOW HIMSELF TO LOSE!
KSSH

HE'D NEVER LET THAT HAPPEN!
OVER MY DEAD BODY, YOU PUNK!!
BOM

READ THIS WAY
PADMM
KWSSH
DAA
SADA-
HARU...
WHAT'S UP?
JIN'S TURNING IT AROUND...

I TOLD YOU I'D WHIP YOUR SCRAWNY LITTLE RUMP!!
!
GAME! SCORE IS 4-ALL!!
OOOOO

AAA
RAA
JIN—!!!
YAMABUKI YAMABUKI
OH MAN! JIN'S TIED THE SCORE!
HE'S VARYING THE RHYTHM...
I THOUGHT OFFENSE WAS THE ONLY WAY HE KNEW HOW TO PLAY...
TAKING MY ADVICE MUST HAVE BEEN HUMILIATING FOR HIM...
LET'S SEE HIM EXECUTE IT!
OOO
I'VE NEVER SEEN YOU SO DETERMINED TO WIN...

"I RECENTLY STARTED PLAYING TENNIS. I WOULD LIKE TO LEARN SOME PUBLIC COURT ETIQUETTE..."

SHINJI AND HAJIME'S LAID-BACK TENNIS CORNER

PART 1

GENIUS 107: AKUTSU'S PRIDE/RYOMA'S COURAGE

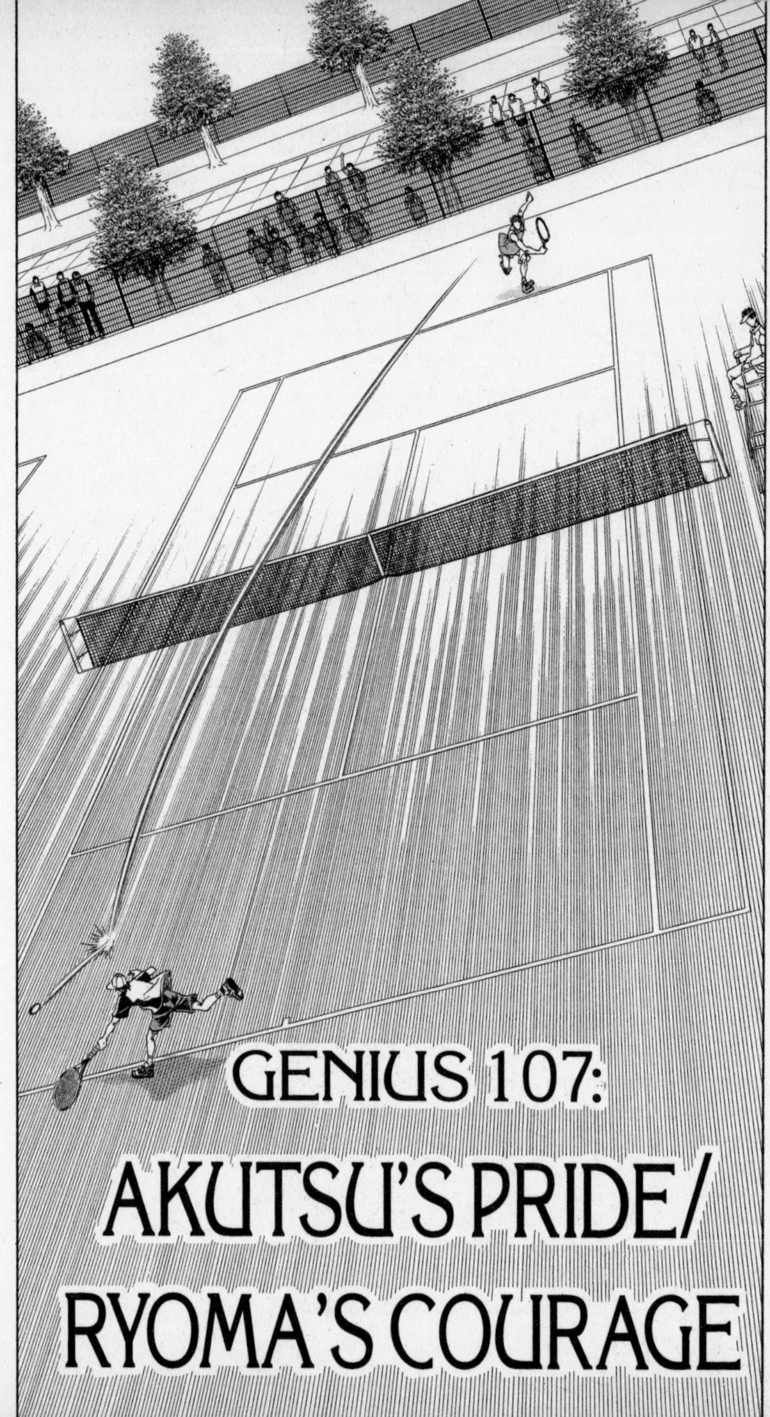
GENIUS 107:
AKUTSU'S PRIDE/
RYOMA'S COURAGE

READ THIS WAY

HF
HF
HF
JIN'S CHANGING TACTICS AND THROWING OFF RYOMA'S RHYTHM!!

THAT OLD FART WAS RIGHT!

JUST BY VARYING THE TEMPO OF MY SHOTS—

—MY DRIVES ARE BECOMING MORE EFFECTIVE!
WHOA— !!
NO!!
HOW ABOUT IT, RYOMA?
STILL THINK YOU CAN OUTWIT JIN?

SSSH

HF

WON'T THIS BOY EVER GIVE UP...?

NYE-HE...

HF

HUH ?!

HE JUST WON'T GO AWAY...

WAAA

NEITHER OF THEM IS LETTING UP!!
HOW WILL THIS MATCH GO DOWN?!
VSSH

READ THIS WAY

OOOO
GO, RYOMA!!
JIN! JIN!
WAAA
DM
SUPER USE-LESS!!
RAAA

RYOMA'S ONE TOUGH BOY...

READ THIS WAY

DG
DUDE ...

IF YOU'D STUCK WITH KARATE, YOU WOULDN'T HAVE TO LOSE TO A TWERP LIKE ME!

SHUT IT!!

EITHER JIN'S PRIDE OR RYOMA'S COURAGE...
...WILL DETERMINE THE OUTCOME OF THIS MATCH!

JIN...

IS TENNIS ANY FUN?

JIN! JIN!

HF

RYOMA! RYOMA!

A A
AND FINAL-LY...
RA
...THEY REACH MATCH POINT...

SEIGAKU
TENNIS CLUB

GENIUS 108: BEYOND VICTORY

READ THIS WAY
JIN! JIN!
OOOO
RYOMA! RYOMA!
RAA
WAAA
SEI-SHUN! SEI-SHUN!
YO, PUNK... I DIDN'T THINK YOU'D STICK AROUND THIS LONG.
YAMA-BUKI! YAMA-BUKI!
THINK MAYBE I'M JUST BUILT DIFFER-ENTLY?
SEI-SHUN! SEI-SHUN!
IT'S MATCH POINT, RYOMA!! GREAT JOB GETTING THIS FAR AGAINST JIN!
TAKE US HOME, RYOMA!! ONE MORE POINT AND WE WIN!!

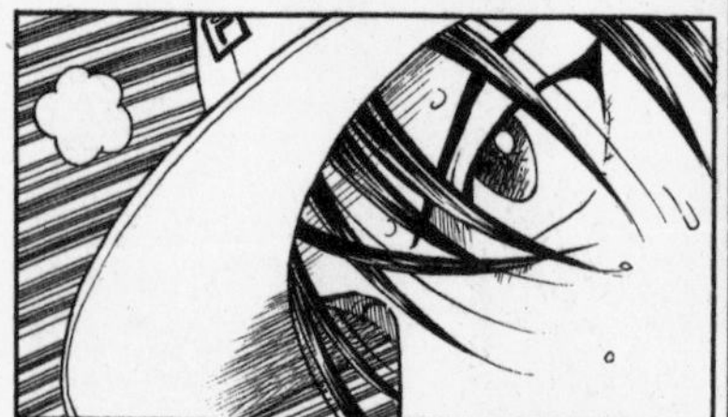

AN ON-THE-RISE SHOT!!

READ THIS WAY
HE'S... HE'S NOT PULLING ANY PUNCHES EVEN AT MATCH POINT!
SEIGAKU
COME AND GET IT, YOU BRAT!!

AAAAGH!!
DSSH
HEH!
THAT'S RIGHT, KEEP WHACKING THAT BALL!!
IT AIN'T GONNA WORK, YA TWIT!!
OOOOOOO

READ THIS WAY
DG
HMM... COME TO THINK OF IT, YOU STILL HAVE A DEBT TO SETTLE!
FOR SPILLING THAT DRINK OVER TAKA'S HEAD...
...AND FOR BEATING UP ARAI!
!
DRIVE A!!
SEIGAKU
WPSH

DON'T EVEN...
I SHUT THAT DOWN EARLIER IN THE MATCH!

VSSH
H-HE GOT IT BACK?!

WHAT—
FROM THAT CLOSE ?!
WH- WHOA ...!

BUT YOU AND I AREN'T SQUARE YET...

YOU HIT ME WITH A ROCK TOO!
!
PUNK !!
DANG! FINISH IT, RYOMA !!

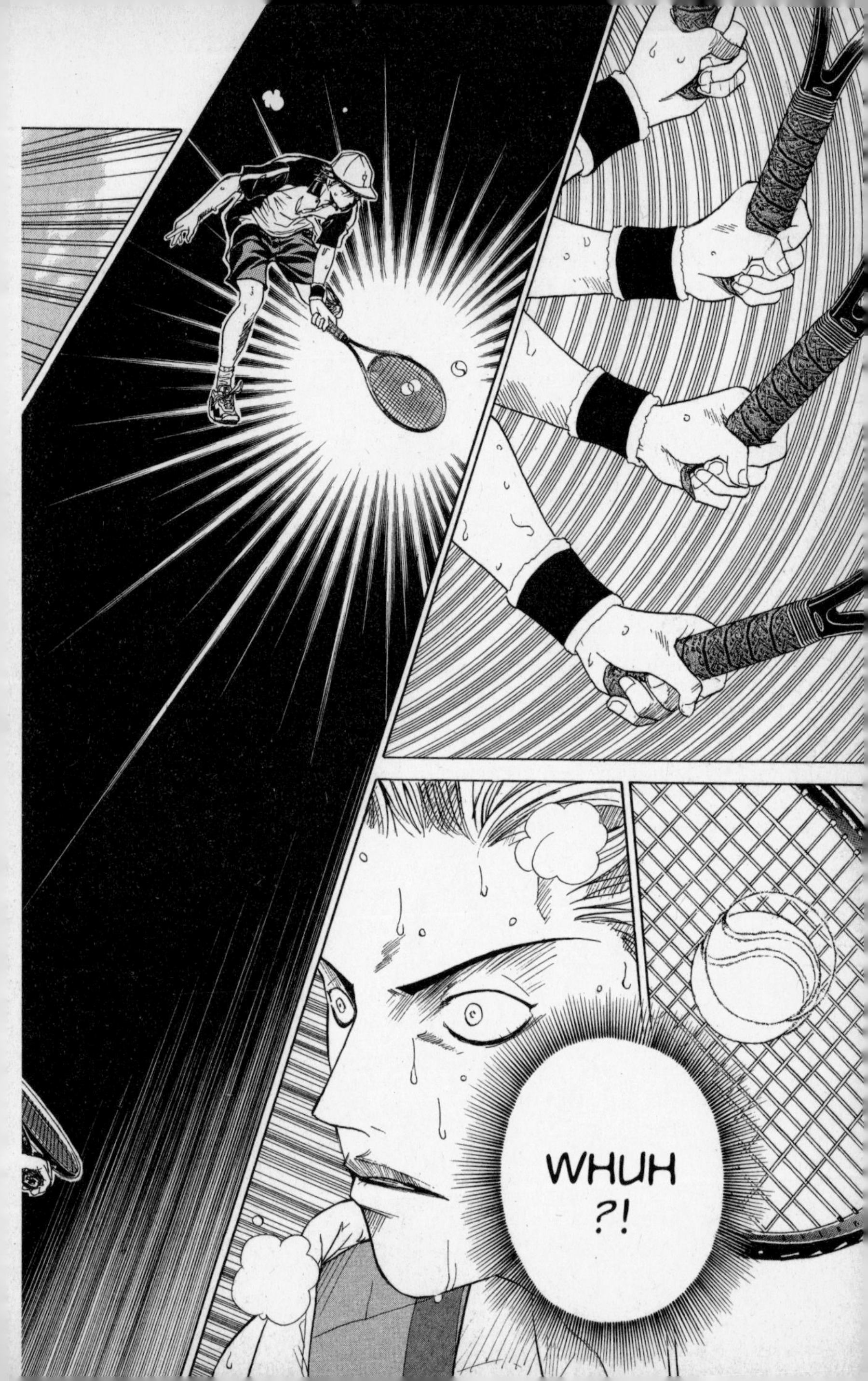
WHUH ?!

READ
THIS
WAY

A DROP VOLLEY...
HOW DARE YOU PULL SOMETHING LIKE THAT NOW...?
TNK
NLOP
ORT

!
DG
DG
DG
DG
WHOA, JIN'S—
SOME-
BODY
SAVE
RYOMA!!
山吹

READ THIS WAY

I WIN!

YOU'RE NO SLOUCH YOURSELF.

HEH ...
BWA-BWA-HAHAHA-HA!!

GAME AND SET! SEISHUN'S ECHIZEN WINS 6 GAMES TO 4!!

WE WON!!
YOU GO, RYOMA!!
WOOHOO! WE WON THE CITY TOURNAMENT!!
THAT KID DID IT!!

YOU WERE SO CLOSE, JIN!!
CLAP
CLAP
CLAP
PSSH
CLAP
JIN...
KE KE
WE MAY HAVE LOST, BUT THERE WAS A LOT THAT YAMABUKI GAINED...
KE KE
NOW JIN CAN FINALLY...

READ THIS WAY

SO, HOW 'BOUT IT? TENNIS ISN'T SO BAD, IS IT?

IT BLOWS!

THAT MATCH ...

...AGAINST THE LITTLE PUNK WAS ENOUGH!

I'M DONE!

.....

IT MAY HAVE BEEN TOO INTENSE FOR HIM...

SCRATCH

SEIGAKU
YEP... THAT BOY COM-PLETELY FOILED IT.

SHINJI AND HAJIME'S
LAID-BACK TENNIS CORNER

1. PLEASE WEAR TENNIS SHOES (ATHLETIC SHOES) INSIDE A TENNIS COURT.

HEELS ARE A NO-NO. TREAT THE COURT WELL.

DO PEOPLE ACTUALLY DO THAT? WOULDN'T IT BE HARD TO RUN AROUND?

AND MAKE SURE YOU WIPE THE SOLES OF YOUR SHOES BEFORE STEPPING ONTO THE COURT, NGYUK-NGYUK.

GENIUS 109: POSSIBILITY

SEARCH

SEARCH

HEY, LOOK!

ISN'T THAT TAKA'S GIRL-FRIEND?

SNEAK

SNEAK

WHAT—

...YUUKI, JIN'S MOTHER.

...NO WAY?!

BUT YOU CALLED HER BY HER FIRST NAME!
SHE GETS UPSET IF I DON'T!
HAHA...
HOW OLD IS SHE?
33.

VONDA
I THINK I KNOW WHY JIN'S THE WAY HE IS...

GENIUS 109: POSSIBILITY

SWITCH
KIKIN
MONDA
6
DUNLOP
FORT

THE TOURNA-MENT RESULTS ARE AS FOLLOWS...
THE FIVE SCHOOLS THAT WILL PLAY IN THE KANTO TOURNAMENT...
...THE JUNIOR HIGH SCHOOL TOKYO CITY TOURNAMENT, BOYS DIVISION...

FIRST, THE CHAMPIONS...
AAAA
SEIGAKU
TENNIS CLUB
SEIGAKU

PA!
SEISHUN ACAD- EMY!!

SEIGAKU
SEIGAKU
SEIGAKU
SEIGAKU
SEIGA

THE RUNNER-UP IS YAMABUKI JUNIOR HIGH!

FINISHING 3RD IS GINKA JUNIOR HIGH SCHOOL, AND IN 4TH PLACE IS FUDOMINE JUNIOR HIGH.
WINNERS OF THE 5TH PLACE CONSOLA-TION MATCH IS...

WA A A A

HYOTEI ACADEMY !!

OF COURSE IT'S US—RIGHT, KABAJI!

MM-HMM...

I'M SLEEPY.

LOOK OUT FOR THAT PLAYER— JIRO!

READ THIS WAY

JIN !!

WHY ARE YOU QUITTING TENNIS?!

PLEASE DON'T QUIT.

TAICHI... IF YOU ASPIRE TO BE LIKE ME, THERE'S NO POSSIBILITY BEYOND THAT.

SNIFF
P-POSSI-BILITY...?

SWH

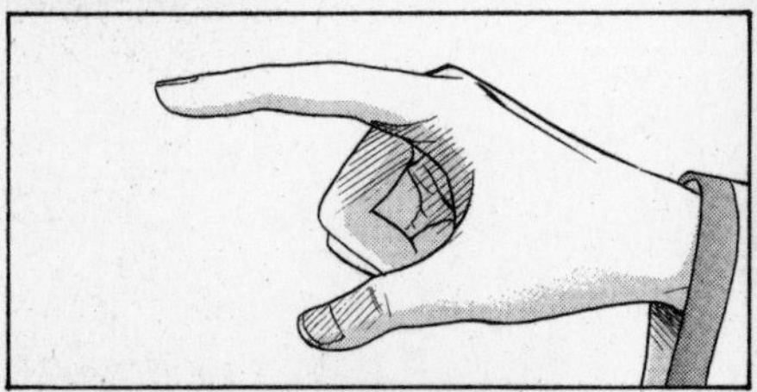

HNH?

I THINK HE'S WAITING FOR YOU.

RYOMA
...

FSSH

SNIFF
SNIFF

LATER.

I-I...
I WANT TO STAND ON THE COURT AS A PLAYER TOO!!
WIPE WIPE
山吹中
I WILL, TOO!!
LATER, YAMABUKI TEAM MANAGER TAICHI DAN SUBMITTED HIS APPLICATION TO CAPTAIN MINAMI...
AND JIN AKUTSU WAS NEVER SEEN ON A TENNIS COURT AGAIN.

-AND WITH THAT...

READ
THIS
WAY

...THE CITY TOURNAMENT CAME TO AN END.

THE PRINCE OF TENNIS THE PRINCE OF TENNIS THE PRINCE OF TENNIS
JIN, I FOUND YOU ♡ I HAD TO COME—
...
SHK
SHK
SHK

GENIUS 110:
MIXED RANKING MATCH

HEHE...
HAVE FUN, RYOMA!
SHF

"IS THIS A DOOR? NO. IT IS A WINDOW."
WHAT A WEIRD QUESTION. GOTTA BE SMART ENOUGH TO NAME IT.

WHOA
MIND IF I SIT NOW, SIR? YOUR PRONUNCIATION ISN'T ALL THAT BAD, THOUGH.
YOU CAN'T BE SERIOUS...

WHAT?
HUH? OH... SURE.

RING
RING

IT'S TRUE—RYOMA'S FLUENT IN ENGLISH!

HEY...
GEEZ ...
CAN WE JUST GET THIS DONE?
YEAH, RYOMA'S RIGHT–
HEE
HEE
GET CRACKING, HORIO–
YELL
YELL
STOP BOSSING US AROUND !!
SHUT UP, BOTH OF YOU!! YOU, AKANE AND SUZUMARI, HOW LONG ARE YOU GALS GONNA CLEAN THE TOP OF THE STAIRS–?!
WE'RE GONNA COLLECT THE TRASH SOON!!
...GRRR.

THIS AREA ISN'T A BREEZE TO CLEAN. THE MUSIC ROOM'S A LOT EASIER.

YEAH, LOOK AT ALL THIS...

LET'S FINISH UP AND GO!

GET OUTTA THE WAY!!

BDG

HEY ?!!

HEY...

D-DUDE!

GYA HAHA, SHOOT IT!!

YOU KICKED UP THE TRASH!

THAT'S WHAT THAT BROOM'S FOR!
YOU GOT A PROBLEM WITH THAT, 7TH GRADER?! HAHAHA!!

R-RYOMA...

CHK

DANG, KAZU'S FREE THROW KEEPS GETTING BETTER!

TELL ME ABOUT IT...

WELL, IT SEEMS THIS YEAR'S 7TH GRADERS DON'T HAVE ANY MANNERS.
YOU BETTER WATCH IT...
DDG
SHUT YOUR TRAP AND KEEP CLEANING!!
DSH

READ THIS WAY

AHAHA, ALL RIGHT! HERE'S MY TENTH IN ROW!!

!
TOK
A TENNIS BALL ...?!
TUP

OH, THERE'S NOTHING TO IT.
WHAT THE HECK, MAN—?!
DID HE HIT THAT WITH A BROOM ???

K-CHK
YES—!! KAZU MAKES THE FIRST BASKET!!
HEH... YOU'RE UP NEXT!

WSSHP

WHOA—
IT'S
IN!!
DDM
I KNOW THE TENNIS BALL'S SMALL, BUT HITTING IT WITH A BROOM?!

COULD I MOVE BACK A LITTLE?

!
IT'S TOO CLOSE.

Y-YOU WHAT ...?

WHOA–
NEITHER
OF THEM IS
MISSING!!

HEY,
CHECK
THIS
OUT!
YAK
YAK YAK
AN 8TH GRADE
BASKETBALL
PLAYER AND A
MYSTERIOUS
7TH GRADE
TENNIS PLAYER
ARE HAVING A
FREE-THROW
SHOOTOUT!!
HF
HF

READ
THIS
WAY

THAT KID'S BEEN TAKING A STEP BACK AFTER EACH SHOT, BUT HE'S SINKING THE BALLS JUST AS ACCURATELY!
YAK
YAK
THAT'S GOTTA PUT PRESSURE ON KAZU...
ZM
M
CRAP... A BASKET-BALL PLAYER...
... CAN'T LOSE AT FREE THROWS ...
...T-TO SOME KID!!

H-HE MISSED !!

GEEZ...!

!

HEY, HOW FAR ARE YOU GOING, RYOMA?

READ THIS WAY
TURN

THAT'S ABOUT THE LENGTH OF THE TENNIS COURT, RIGHT?
ZMM
I THINK YOU'LL BE NEEDING THIS...

THANKS, MOMO.
FFF

THAT'S THE TENNIS TEAM'S FAMOUS 7TH GRADE STARTER!!
WSHIPP
W-WOW...
HE GOT IT IN WITHOUT EVEN TOUCHING THE NET!

YOU'VE GOT A WAYS TO GO!

SHINJI AND HAJIME'S
LAID-BACK TENNIS CORNER

ETIQUETTE

2. IF YOUR BALL LANDS ON THE ADJACENT COURT, DO NOT RETRIEVE THE BALL WHILE THEIR BALL IS IN PLAY.

VROOM

WE'RE HERE AT SEI-SHUN!

HURRY, SAORI!

WAIT UP, MR. INOUE!!

GENIUS 111: INTRA-SQUAD RANKING MATCHES

THE KANTO TOURNAMENT STARTERS WILL BE DECIDED TODAY!!
JUNE INTRA-SQUAD
KAWAMURA
KAIDO
NISHI
TAKASHI KAWAMURA (9TH)
KAORU KAIDO (8TH)
HIDETO NISHI (9TH)
DAISUKE HAYASHI (8TH)
MANABU NINOSE (8TH)
YUUYA NAKAHAMA (8TH)
JUNE INTR
ECHIZEN
BLOCK D PRELIMINARY

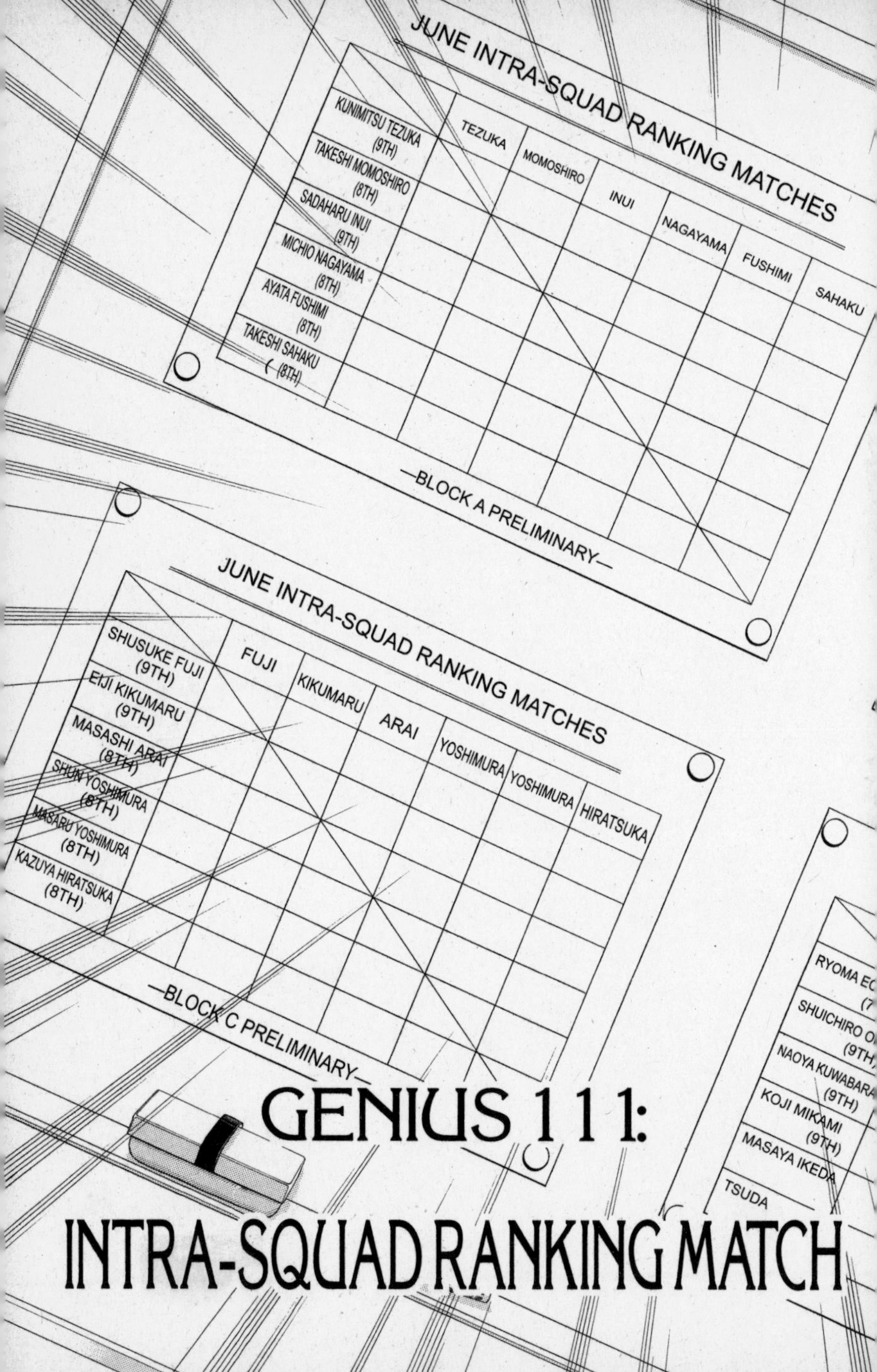

GENIUS 111: INTRA-SQUAD RANKING MATCH

OOOO
IF YOU THOUGHT THE CURRENT STARTERS CAN MAKE IT, YOU'RE SADLY MISTAKEN.

HMMF

WHAT— SO YOU'RE SAYING IF YOU'RE NOT IN THE TOP TWO OF BLOCKS A, B, C, AND D...
...EVEN THE CURRENT STARTERS WON'T GO TO THE KANTO TOURNA-MENT?
THAT'S ROUGH—!!
TUP
ON THE FLIPSIDE, IT'S AN OPPORTUNITY FOR ANYBODY TO BECOME A STARTER...

READ THIS WAY

AS USUAL, IT'S ALL THE 8TH AND 9TH GRADERS, WITH RYOMA BEING THE ONLY 7TH GRADER IN THE BUNCH.

I WISH I COULD PLAY IN IT.

RYOMA'S THE ONLY 7TH GRADE EXCEPTION...

BUT IN SEPTEMBER, WHICH IS ONLY THREE MONTHS AWAY, YOU GUYS WILL BE PLAYING IN IT TOO.

WOW, REALLY...?

MY GAME IS ON!!
EEEK
GOOD—!!
YAAH!!
BMM

WHR
WHR
WHR
OOOOO
SHUI-CHIRO'S FAMOUS ...
WHR
WHR
MOON VOLLEY !!
AWESOME ...!!
HE'S AIMING RIGHT FOR THE LINE!!

TOO BAD, MY REGRETS ...
CATCH YOU NEXT WEEK–!!
BM
THERE IT IS... EIJI'S ACRO-BATIC PLAY!!
OOOO

BOOM
NK
MY DUNK'S IN GOOD FORM TODAY.
CHNG
YAAH !!

UH-HUH... OURS TOO...

CAN WE KEEP UP WITH THEM?

AND THE STARTERS RACKED UP THE WINS.

RAAA

DMM

DG

GAME AND SET! CAPTAIN TEZUKA WINS!!

WAAAA

MAN, HE'S GOOD— HE DIDN'T LOSE A SINGLE POINT!

GOOD GAME!

CLAP

CLAP

SWISH
THERE YOU HAVE IT— KAORU'S SNAKE!!
HFF
BLECH... HOW BORING!
THAT GUY'S FROM BLOCK D...

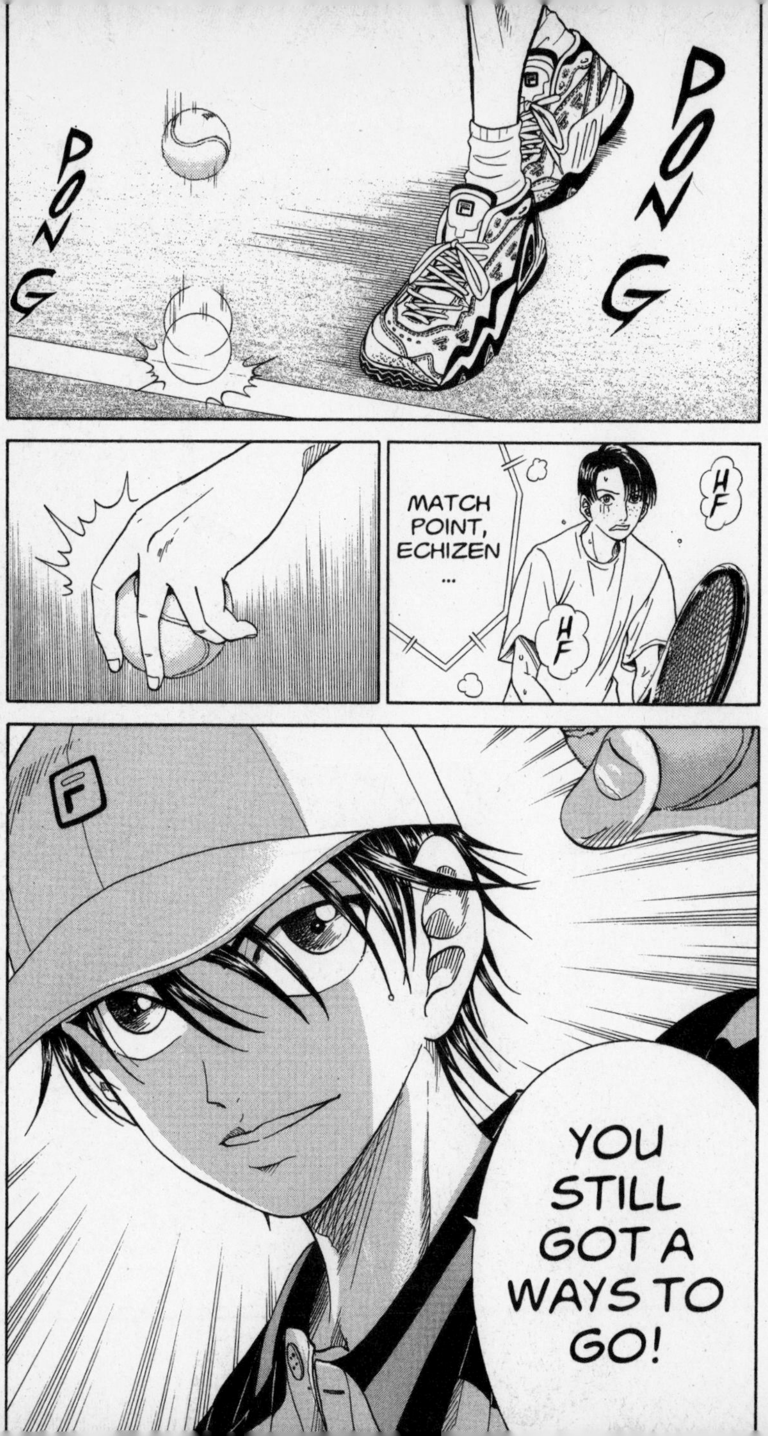

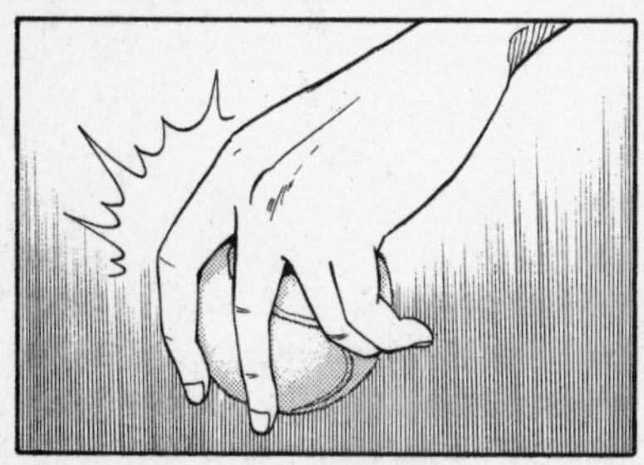

YOU STILL GOT A WAYS TO GO!

TWIST SERVE !!

FWHH

AYA AAH !!

GAME AND SET!!

ECHIZEN WINS!!

TUP

TUP

IT'S UNFORTU-NATE THAT YOU HAD TO PLAY ME, MASAYA.

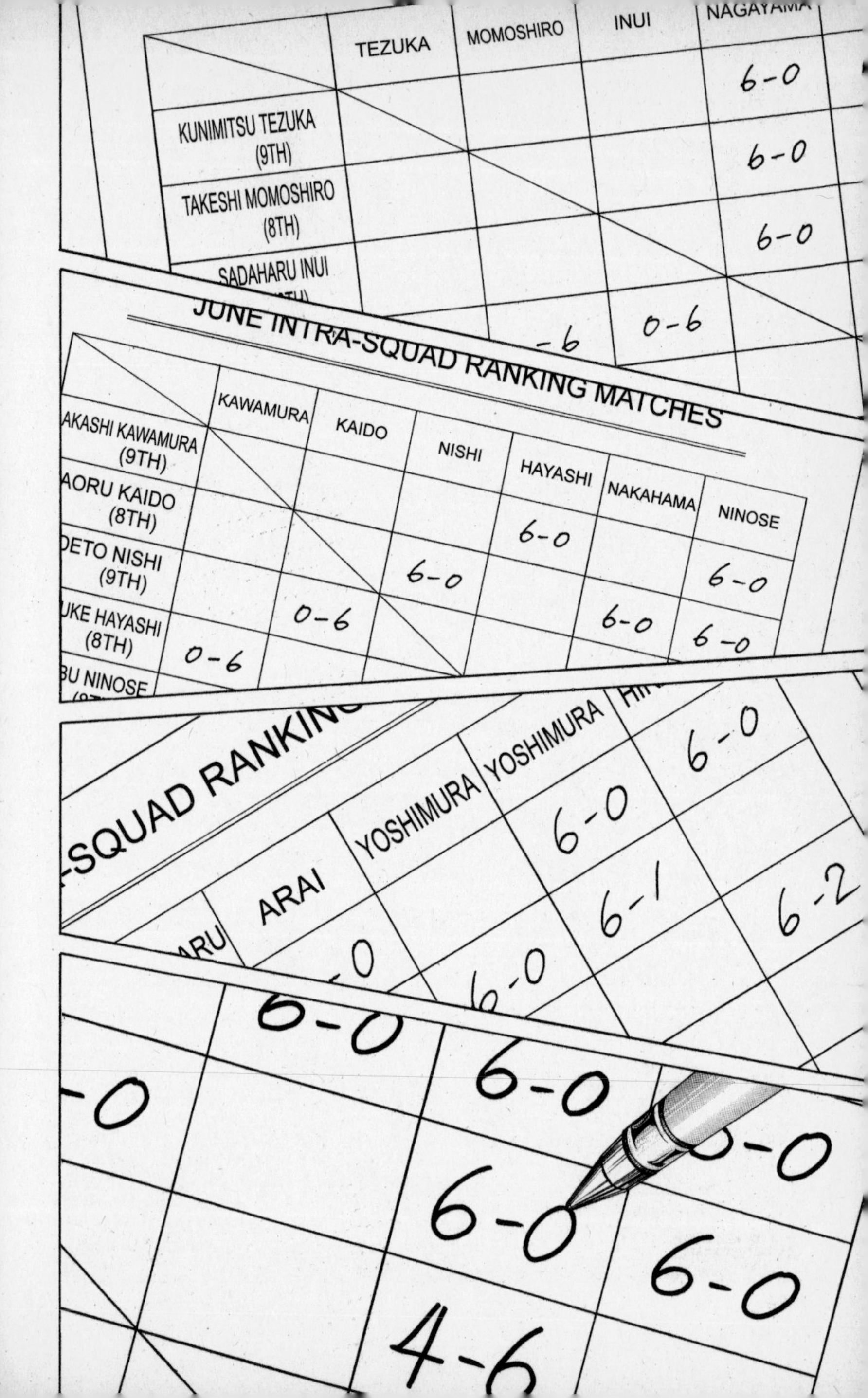

TEZUKA
MOMOSHIRO
INUI
NAGAYAMA
KUNIMITSU TEZUKA (9TH)
TAKESHI MOMOSHIRO (8TH)
SADAHARU INUI
6-0
6-0
6-0
0-6
JUNE INTRA-SQUAD RANKING MATCHES
KAWAMURA
KAIDO
NISHI
HAYASHI
NAKAHAMA
NINOSE
AKASHI KAWAMURA (9TH)
AORU KAIDO (8TH)
DETO NISHI (9TH)
UKE HAYASHI (8TH)
BU NINOSE
6-0
6-0
6-0
0-6
6-0
6-0
0-6
-SQUAD RANKING
ARAI
YOSHIMURA
YOSHIMURA
6-0
6-0
6-1
6-2
6-0
6-0
6-0
6-0
6-0
4-6

THE PROBABILITY OF A DOWN-THE-LINE SHOT ON THE RIGHT IS 100%....

VSSH
GAME AND SET. INUI WINS 6-0.
OOOOO
WITH YOUR LEG STRENGTH, YOU'LL BE 45 CM SHORT...
FORMER SEISHUN NO. 3 SINGLES PLAYER... DATA TENNIS IS ALIVE AND WELL... SADAHARU.
LOOKS LIKE IT.

ONE INTRA-SQUAD RA... ...ES

	TEZUKA	MOMOSHIRO	INUI	NAGAYAMA	FUSHIMI	SAHA
KUNIMITSU TEZUKA (9TH)				6-0	6-0	
TAKESHI MOMOSHIRO (8TH)				6-0	6-0	6-0
SADAHARU INUI (9TH)				6-0		6-0
MICHIO NAGAYAMA (8TH)	0-6	0-6	0-6			
AYATA FUSHIMI (8TH)	0-6	0-6				
KESHI SAHAKU (8TH)		0-6	0-6			

—BLOCK A PRELIM...

THE PRINCE OF TENNIS THE PRINCE OF TENNIS THE PRINCE OF TENNIS
DO YOU GUYS REMEMBER US—?
SHIBA.
INOUE.
I'M WITH PRO TENNIS MONTHLY.
PRO TENNIS MONTHLY
6

WAAA
AAA
DMMM
SHUSUKE FUJI (9TH)
EIJI KIKUMARU (9TH)
MASASHI ARAI (8TH)
0-6
GAME AND SET. KIKUMARU WINS 6-0!!
PEACE, PEACE, PEACE—
DUNLOP
GENIUS 112: BLOCK A

A
GAWD... EIJI'S ON TODAY—
HF
HF
YOU LOST WITH GRACE, ARAI.
SHUT UP!
A
HF
WHEN ARE WE EVER GONNA BE START-ERS?
TELL ME ABOUT IT.
A
AAA
.....
SHUT
OOOH
AA

GENIUS 112:
BLOCK A
SEIGAKU
TENNIS CLUB
SEIGAKU
SEIGAKU
SEIGAKU
PUMA

THE JUNE INTRA-SQUAD RANKING MATCHES WERE HELD TO DECIDE...
...THE START-ERS FOR THE KANTO TOURNA-MENT–

READ THIS WAY

THE CURRENT STARTERS BREAK OUT THEIR SKILLS AND PREDICT-ABLY WIN...

HF
HF
DG DG
SEIGAKU
YAH !!
BMM
O
OOOO
SHUICHIRO...
WHAT TENAC-ITY...
HF

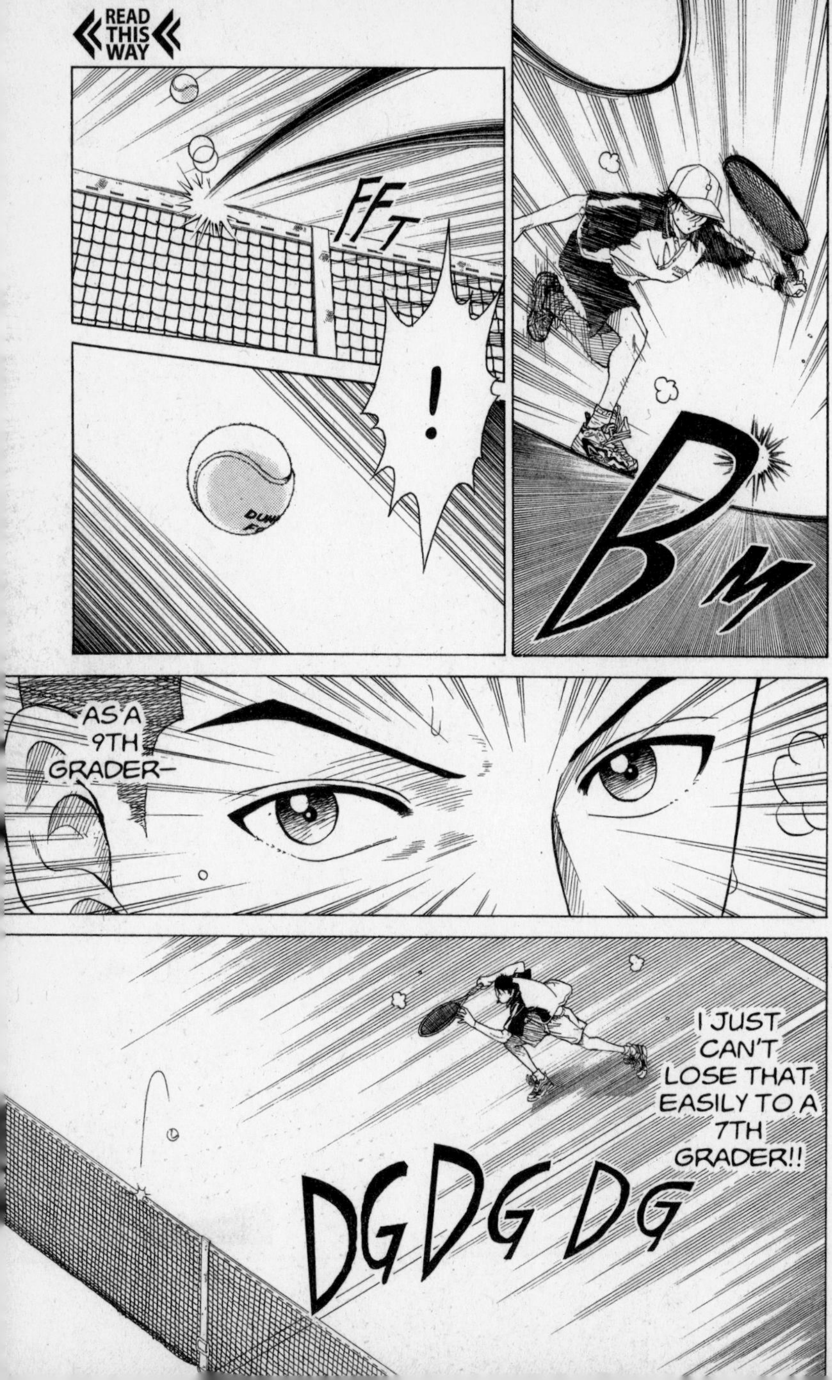

READ THIS WAY

BM

FFT

!

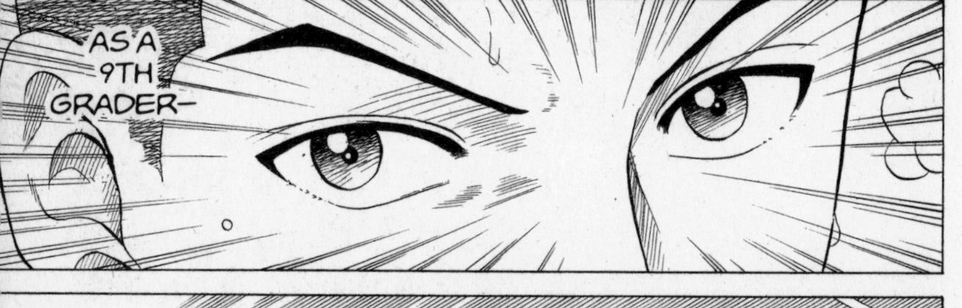

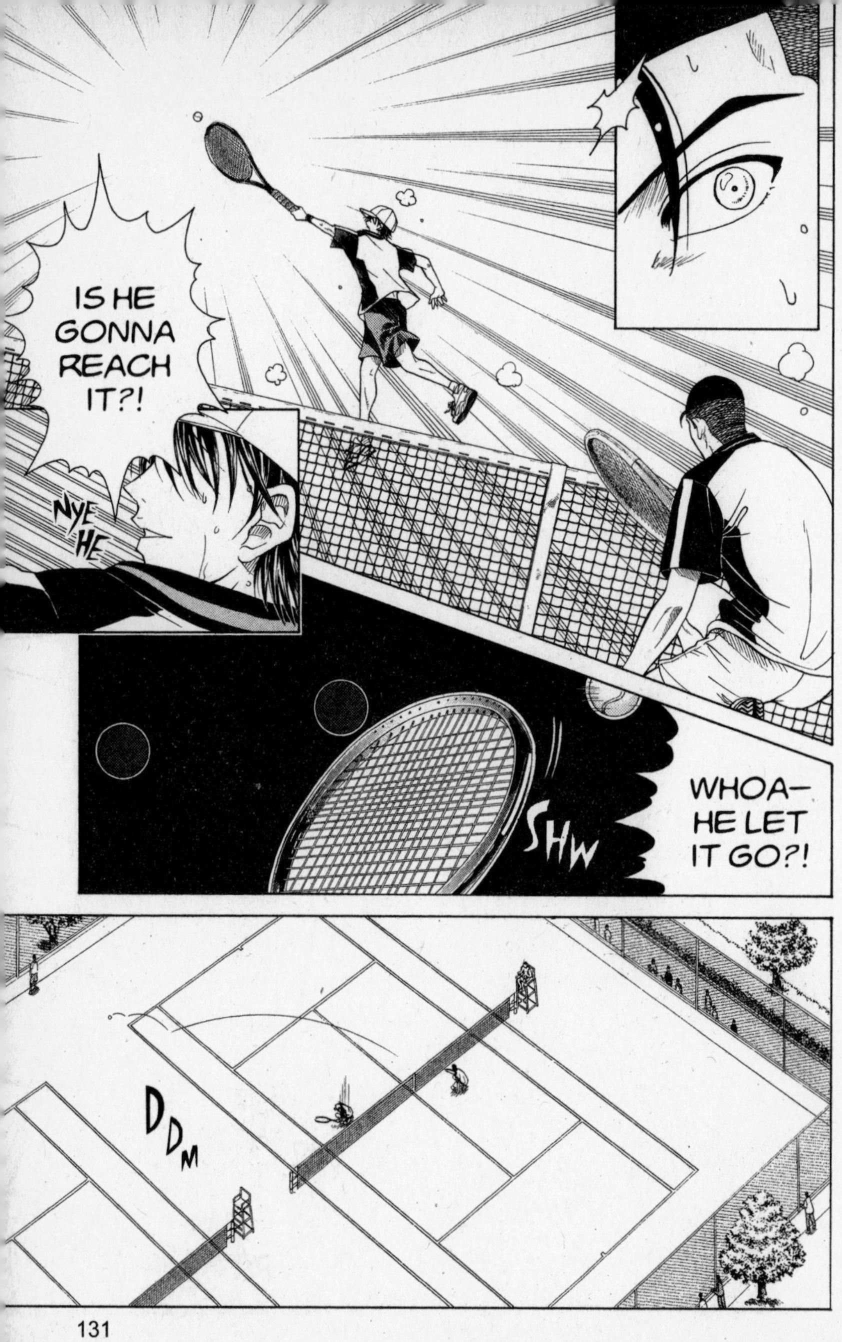

IS HE GONNA REACH IT?!

NYE HE

WHOA- HE LET IT GO?!

SHW

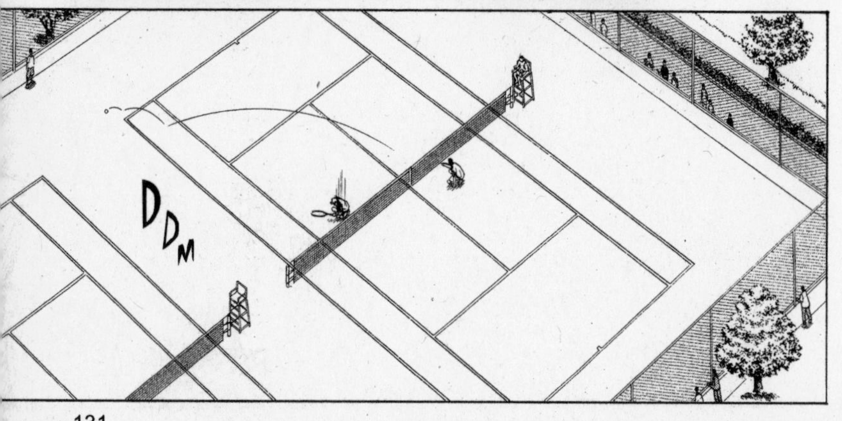

O-OUT...

HF

HF

GAME AND SET. ECHIZEN WINS 6-3!!
NICE GOING, RYOMA!
THAT'S A SWEEP! HE'S A STARTER AGAIN!
PHEW— YOU'RE GOOD, RYOMA...
YOU TOTALLY GOT ME.
I KEPT MY STARTER SPOT WITH JUST ONE LOSS TOO.
CONGRATULATIONS!

READ THIS WAY

SHF SHF
YOU REALLY ARE GOOD, RYOMA!
CONGRATULATIONS! YOU FINISHED FIRST IN BLOCK D.

THE STARTERS ARE WINNING IN THE OTHER BLOCKS TOO!
REALLY ...

BUT BLOCK A IS GETTING INTERESTING...

IT'S CAPTAIN TEZUKA AND MOMO...
AND DESPITE LOSING HIS SPOT AS A STARTER, THERE'S SADAHARU...
IT'S A THREE-WAY STRUGGLE!

HEY WAIT... LISTEN TO ME, RYOMA!
TUP

JUNE INTRA-SQUAD RANKING MATCHES
TEZUKA MOMOSHIRO INUI NAGAYAMA FUSHIMI SAHAKU
KUNIMITSU TEZUKA (9TH) 6-1 6-0 6-0 6-0
TAKESHI MOMOSHIRO (8TH) 1-6 2-6 6-0 6-0 6-0
SADAHARU INUI (9TH) 6-2 6-0 6-0 6-0
MICHIO NAGAYAMA (8TH) 0-6 0-6 0-6 4-6 6-3
AYATA FUSHIMI (8TH) 0-6 0-6 0-6 6-4 6-1
TAKESHI SAHAKU (8TH) 0-6 0-6 0-6 3-6 1-6
—BLOCK A PRELIMINAR
WHAT ?!
MOMO'S ...
...LOSING!
2-6
6

READ THIS WAY

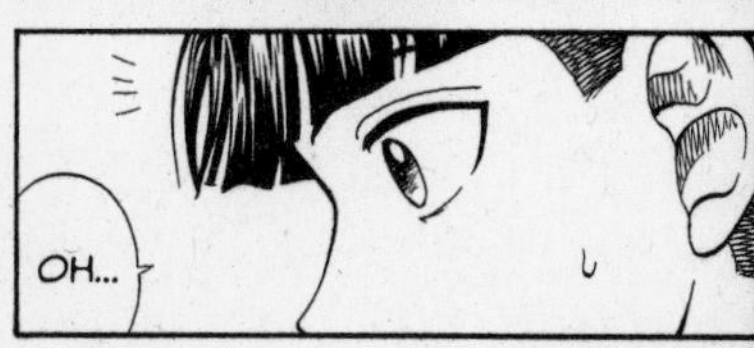

	TEZUKA	MOMOSHIRO	INUI
KUNIMITSU TEZUKA (9TH)		6-1	
TAKESHI MOMOSHIRO (8TH)	1-6		2-6
SADAHARU INUI (9TH)		6-2	
MICHIO NAGAYAMA (8TH)	0-6	0-6	0-6
		0-6	0-6

FOR THE PAST TWO MONTHS, DURING THE DISTRICT PRELIMS AND CITY TOURNAMENT...

SADAHARU WASN'T JUST SUPPORTING US BY COLLECTING DATA ON OTHER SCHOOLS.

WHAT ...?

HOW DOES IT FEEL ...

...BEING OBSERVED ON THE SLY FOR TWO WHOLE MONTHS?

READ THIS WAY

T-THIS IS GREAT, SHIBA...

SCRITCH

WE GOT A STORY! THIS IS A STORY!

SCRITCH

WITHIN THE SAME SCHOOL...

...A BATTLE SO FIERCE...

I FINALLY HAVE ENOUGH DATA...
I'M WINNING THIS TIME, KUNIMITSU!

SHF
ONE-SET MATCH... INUI TO SERVE!
GULP
BEGIN PLAY!!

THE PRINCE OF TENNIS THE PRINCE OF TENNIS THE PRINCE OF TENNIS
A GUY WHO HASN'T PLAYED IN A WHILE...
A GUY WHO HASN'T AP-PEARED IN A WHILE ...
SHOWDOWN!!

GENIUS 113: DATA DOES NOT LIE

GENIUS 113:
DATA DOES NOT LIE

THERE IT IS— THE POWER SERVE!!

POM

A LOW DOWN-THE-LINE SHOT FROM THE RIGHT WITH SOME TOPSPIN ON IT...
I'D SAY ABOUT A 17-DEGREE ANGLE...
DG
HERE IT COMES, HERE IT COMES... DATA TENNIS!!
POM
HE WAS RIGHT! IT'S A DOWN-THE-LINE SHOT FROM THE RIGHT!
IT'S LIKE A SERIOUS GAME OF CHESS!

READ THIS WAY

TMP

!

NICE LOB!! CAPTAIN TEZUKA'S TOTALLY CHILL!!

PUMA
I CAN MAKE IT!!
SMASH
HE GOT TO THE LOB?!

READ
THIS
WAY

I SEE...

STUFF SADAHARU NEVER HAD BEFORE...
LEG STRENGTH TO LEAP... AND POWER.

SEIGAKU

READ THIS WAY

TH-THAT'S... CAPTAIN TEZUKA'S BEST WEAPON...

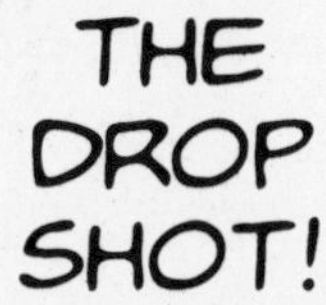

HITTING IT IN THE SAME MANNER AS A NORMAL SHOT...

...DISGUISES IT PERFECTLY.

6
DUNLOP
FORT

SADA-HARU ANTICI-PATED IT?!
BUT TO GET TO IT FROM WHERE HE WAS—?!
THE PROBA-BILITY OF A DROP SHOT IS 92%...
LEG SPRING AND SPEED...
GAME, INUI!!
DM

WOW—
THIS IS
A TOP-
CALIBER
MATCH!!

HE
RETURNED
CAPTAIN
KUNIMITSU'S
DROP
SHOT?!

OOOO

NOT ONLY DID YOU ANALYZE THE DATA...
LOOKS LIKE YOU POLISHED ONE MORE THING, SADAHARU.
I FELT LIKE AIMING HIGHER.

HE DOUBLED THE TRAINING REGIMEN HE ASSIGNED ME.

KAORU...

HMPH

TAP

IT WAS 2.25 TIMES MORE, TO BE EXACT.

HUH? WHAT? WASN'T KAORU PRACTICING THREE TIMES MORE THAN USUAL?

2.25 TIMES MORE THAN THAT...

READ THIS WAY

OOO
I SEE... HE EVEN WORKED ON HIS BODY.

THAT'S RIGHT! UNTIL NOW, HE WAS ABLE TO PREDICT HIS OPPONENTS' SHOTS BY USING HIS DATA...
...BUT HE LACKED THE SPRINTING CAPACITY AND POWER TO RETURN THE SHOTS.

SADA-HARU'S DATA TENNIS IS STILL EVOLVING!

WAAAA
I GOTTA WARN YOU, HE'S GOOD...

POM
GAME SCORE IS 3-ALL!!
OOOO
HEY! THAT'S AN INTRA-SQUAD RANKING MATCH!
YAK
HAS ANYBODY EVER TAKEN THREE GAMES OFF OF CAPTAIN TEZUKA?
YAK
MUMBLE
MUMBLE
MUMBLE
I DIDN'T KNOW HE WAS THIS GOOD...

READ THIS WAY

PROBABILITY OF A CROSS-COURT SHORT IS 100%...

TOK

GEEZ, SADAHARU'S GOT NO WEAKNESS!!

HE'S FLAWLESS!!

OO

KUNIMITSU...

DATA DOESN'T LIE...

テニスの王子様
THE PRINCE OF TENNIS
TM

GENIUS 114:
SEIGAKU
SUPERIOR
DATA TENNIS

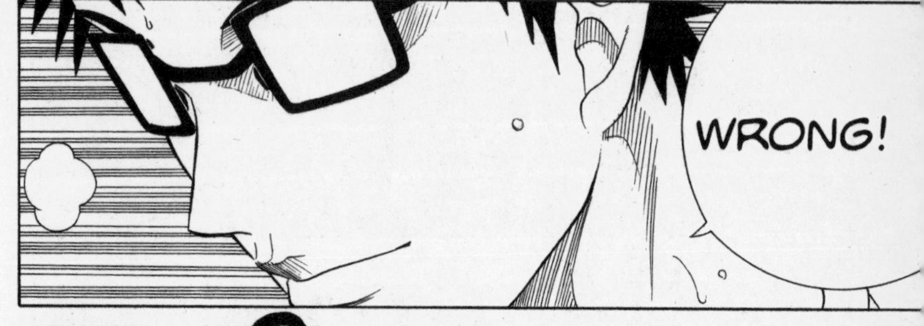
WRONG!

BAM

OOOO
GAME INUI. SCORE IS 4-3!!

SADA-HARU IS PLAYING SO WELL!!

RAAA
I BARELY SAW HIM PRACTICE AFTER HE LOST HIS SPOT AS A STARTER. HE WAS ALWAYS HELPING TO COACH US.
I DIDN'T KNOW HE WAS WORKING SO HARD...

OOO
I'M ACTUALLY NOT SURPRISED THAT SADAHARU'S PLAYING EFFORTLESSLY.
HIS PHYSICAL STRENGTH HAS IMPROVED.
HE WAS TALL TO BEGIN WITH—GOOD FOR TENNIS...
THERE WAS ALWAYS ROOM FOR HIM TO IMPROVE.

IT JUST SHOWS HIS DISAP-POINTMENT OVER LOSING TO SOME-BODY...

OOO
AAA

SHW

HEY, KUNIMITSU... WHEN YOU HIT A DROP SHOT, YOUR RACKET HEAD DROPS 3.2mm...

SINCE SADAHARU CAME TO THIS SCHOOL, HOW MANY TIMES HAVE THESE TWO PLAYED EACH OTHER?

INCLUDING OFFICIAL MATCHES, IT MUST BE AT LEAST 20... NO, 30...

SADAHARU NEVER BEAT KUNIMITSU...

SEIGAKU

BAM
TOK
HARD WORK AND DETERMINATION...
PUMA

...AT TIMES SURPASSES SKILL.

TH- THIS IS SUPERIOR DATA TENNIS!!

IT'S BREAK POINT. SADAHARU'S UP 4-3 AND LEADING THIS GAME 30-40...

IF HE BREAKS CAPTAIN TEZUKA'S SERVICE GAME, IT'LL BE 5-3.

A COMMANDING LEAD FOR SADAHARU!

HF

SHW

IS CAPTAIN TEZUKA GOING TO...

SHW

..LOSE
?!

IT'S TRUE— TENNIS ISN'T DECIDED JUST BY THE SUPERIORITY OF ONE'S SKILL.
ISN'T THAT WHAT YOU SAID BEFORE, KUNIMITSU ...?
SEIGAKU

SINCE THAT DAY, SADAHARU WAS DETERMINED TO REGAIN HIS STARTER SPOT FOR THE KANTO TOURNAMENT...
HE PRACTICED, COLLECTED DATA, AND CAME UP WITH A STRATEGY FOR TODAY.
HE EVEN BEAT MOMO. HIS DESIRE TO BECOME A STARTER ONCE AGAIN IS ENOUGH TO INSPIRE ANYBODY...

BUT FOR KUNI-MITSU TO BE COR-NERED BY A TEAM-MATE...

B
DEUCE!!
OH, DID KUNIMITSU SCORE A POINT ...?
HM...
... HUH?
SEIGAKU

WH-
WHAT
THE
HECK IS
GOING
ON?!

HF

HF

KUNI-MITSU... WHAT WAS THAT?

TUP
C'MON SADAHARU—THE MATCH ISN'T OVER YET. LET'S KEEP GOING!

TUP
Twist-Resistant
SEIGAKU
TENNIS CLUB
PRO LIGHT
TO BE CONTINUED...

SHINJI AND HAJIME'S
LAID-BACK TENNIS CORNER

3. MAINTAIN THE COURTS BY BRUSHING AND/OR SWEEPING THE LINES REGULARLY!!

※BESIDES THESE, MAKE SURE TO READ THE RULES POSTED AT THE TENNIS COURTS! WANG CHUNG, EVERYBODY!

テニスの王子様
THE PRINCE OF TENNIS™

Thank you for reading Prince of Tennis Vol. 13.
By the time Vol. 13 comes out, it should be spring, the season of the new school semester.
I've been receiving a lot of letters saying, "I started playing tennis after reading The Prince of Tennis." As its author, I couldn't be happier!! At first it may just be picking up balls or practicing your form, but please keep it up. One day you will play a match and feel great. Playing sports is wonderful!!
In this volume, I dedicated a section on public tennis court etiquette. Each court has its own rules, though, so please ask the attendant. Try to enjoy tennis with everybody there.
We received so many submissions for the "Kunimitsu Tezuka 9th Grade, Class 1 Classmate Sign-up Contest" (that was introduced in the last volume) that we couldn't compile all of them for this volume. To those of you who may have been anxiously waiting for the results, I'm very sorry!! ← BOW Sorry...
And, to the fans who sent in Valentine's Day chocolates, even the editors were shocked at the amount they received. And for all the letters to the characters, thank you very much! You wouldn't believe the amount that was sent in!! My workspace is filled with the sweet scent of chocolate. We still haven't counted all of them yet either, so please be patient.

I write this in every volume, but every letter I receive from the fans fills me with a sense of gratitude. Saying "thank you" in every volume doesn't capture how much I appreciate all of it. I regret not being able to respond to each and every letter... I hope to keep doing my best using everybody's strong support as inspiration! Thank you so much!!

Well then, keep supporting Prince of Tennis and Ryoma!!
I'll see you in the next volume.

テニスの王子様 ★
T. Konomi
2002.3.13

Send fan letters to: VIZ Media, LLC P.O. Box 77010 San Francisco, CA 94107 Attention: The Prince of Tennis

In the Next Volume...

The intra-squad match between Kunimitsu and Sadaharu of Seishun Academy reaches a dizzying climax, and people begin to realize that Kunimitsu's skills are way beyond that of an average junior high school player...

Available in July 2006

ONE PIECE
ONE PIECE

SUBSCRIBE TODAY & BECOME A MEMBER OF THE SHONEN JUMP SUBSCRIBER CLUB...
You'll get:
*Access to Exclusive Online Content!
*50% Savings Off the Newsstand Price!
*Exclusive Premiums!
All this available ONLY to Subscribers!
SHONEN JUMP
THE WORLD'S MOST POPULAR MANGA ™
FILL OUT THE SUBSCRIPTION CARD ON THE OTHER SIDE, OR SUBSCRIBE ONLINE AT:
www.shonenjump.com